THE ALCHEMY
OF HAPPINESS

AL GHAZZALI

translated by
CLAUD FIELD

British Library Cataloguing in Publication Data

A catalogue record for this book is available from the British Library

ISBN-13: 978-1-908388-43-8

Printed and bound in Great Britain by Lightning Souce UK Ltd., 6 Precedent Drive, Rooksley, Milton Keynes MK13 8PR.

Cover Illustration: *The Prophet Elias and Khadir at the Fountain of Life*. Timurid Dynasty (15th century)

CONTENTS

EDITORIAL NOTE

The object of the Editors of this series is a very definite one. They desire above all things that, in their humble way, these books shall be the ambassadors of good-will and understanding between East and West - the old world of Thought and the new of Action. In this endeavour, and in their own sphere, they are but followers of the highest example in the land. They are confident that a deeper knowledge of the great ideals and lofty philosophy of Oriental thought may help to a revival of that true spirit of Charity which neither despises nor fears the nations of another creed and colour. Finally, in thanking press and public for the very cordial reception given to the "Wisdom of the East" Series, they wish to state that no pains have been spared to secure the best specialists for the treatment of the various subjects at hand.

L. Cranmer-Byng

S.A.Kapadia

Northbrook Society
185 Piccadilly, W.

PREFACE

Renan, whose easy-going mind was the exact antithesis to the intense earnestness of Ghazzali, calls him "the most original mind among Arabian philosophers."[1] Notwithstanding this, his fame as a philosopher has been greatly overshadowed by Avicenna, his predecessor, and Averroes, his successor and opponent. It is a significant fact that the Encyclopædia Britannica devotes five columns to each of the others and only a column and a half to Ghazzali. Yet it is doubtful whether it is as a philosopher that be would have wished to be chiefly remembered. Several of his works, it is true, are polemics against the philosophers, especially his Tehafot-al-falasifa, or "Destruction of the philosophers," and, as Solomon Munk says in his Melanges de philosophie Juive et Arabe, Ghazzali dealt "a fatal blow" to Arabian philosophy in the East, from which it never recovered, though it revived for a while in Spain and culminated in Averroes. Philosopher and sceptic as he was by nature, Ghazzali's chief work was that of a theologian, moralist, and mystic, though his mysticism was strongly balanced by common sense. He had, as he tells us in his Confessions, experienced "conversion"; God had arrested him "on the edge of the fire," and thenceforth what Browning says of the French poet, Rene Gentilhomme, was true of him:

> *Human praises scare*
> *Rather than soothe ears all a-tingle yet*
> *With tones few hear and live, and none forget.*

In the same work he tells us that one of his besetting weaknesses had been the craving for applause, and in his Ihya-ul-ulum ("Revival of the Religious Sciences") he devotes a long chapter to the dangers involved in a love of notoriety and the cure for it.

After his conversion he retired into religious. seclusion for eleven years at Damascus (a corner of the mosque there still bears his name - "The Ghazzali Corner") and Jerusalem, where he gave himself up to intense and prolonged meditation. But he was too noble a character to concentrate himself entirely on his own soul and its eternal

prospects. The requests of his children - and other family affairs of which we have no exact information - caused him to return home. Besides this, the continued progress of the Ismailians (connected with the famous Assassins), the spread of irreligious doctrines and the increasing. religious indifference of the masses not only filled Ghazzali and his Sufi friends with profound grief, but determined them to stem the evil with the whole force of their philosophy, the ardour of vital conviction, and the authority of noble example.

In his autobiography referred to above Ghazzali tells us that, after emerging from a state of Pyrrhonic scepticism, he had finally arrived at the conclusion that the mystics were on the right path and true "Arifin," or Knowers of God.[2] But in saying this he meant those Sufis whose mysticism did not carry them into extravagant utterances like that of Mansur Hallaj, who was crucified at Bagdad (A.D. 922) for exclaiming "I am the Truth, or God." In his Ihya-ul-ulum Ghazzali says: "The matter went so far that certain persons boasted of a union with the Deity, and that in His unveiled presence they beheld Him, and enjoyed familiar converse with Him, saying, "Thus it was spoken unto us and thus we speak." Bayazid Bistami (ob. A. D. 875) is reported to have exclaimed, "Glory be to me!" This style of discourse exerts a very pernicious influence on the common people. Some husbandmen indeed, letting their farms run to waste, set up similar pretensions for themselves; for human nature is pleased with maxims like these, which permit one to neglect useful labour with the idea of acquiring spiritual purity through the attainment of certain mysterious degrees and qualities. This notion is productive of great injury, so that the death of one of these foolish babblers would be a greater benefit to the cause of true religion than the saving alive of ten of them."

For himself Ghazzali was a practical mystic. His aim was to make men better by leading them from a merely notional acquiescence in the stereotyped creed of Islam to a real knowledge of God. The first four chapters of The Alchemy of Happiness are a commentary on the famous verse in the Hadis (traditional sayings of Muhammad), "He who knows himself knows God." He is especially scornful of the parrotlike repetition of orthodox phrases. Thus alluding to the almost hourly use by Muhammadans of the phrase, "I take refuge in God" (*Na`udhib`illah!*), Ghazzali says, in the *Ihya-ul-ulum*: "Satan laughs at such pious ejaculations. Those who utter them are like a man who should meet a lion in a desert, while there is a fort at no great distance, and, when he sees the evil beast, should stand exclaiming, 'I take refuge in that fortress,' without moving a step towards it. What will such an ejaculation profit him? In the same way the mere exclamation, 'I take refuge in God,' will not protect thee from the terrors of His judgment unless thou really take refuge in Him." It is related of some unknown Sufi that when, asked for a definition of religious sincerity he drew a red-hot piece of iron out of a blacksmith's forge, and said, "Behold it!" This "red-hot" sincerity is certainly characteristic of Ghazzali, and there is no wonder that he did not admire his contemporary, Omar Khayyam.

The little picture of the lion and the fort in the above passage is a small instance of another conspicuous trait in Ghazzali's mind - his turn for allegory. Emerson says, "Whoever thinks intently will find an image more or less luminous rise in his mind." In Ghazzali's writings many such images arise, some grotesque and some beautiful. His allegory of the soul as a fortress beleaguered by the "armies of Satan" is a striking anticipation of the Holy War of Bunyan. The greatest of all the Sufi poets, Jalaluddin Rumi, born a century after Ghazzali's death (A.D. 1207), has paid him the compliment of incorporating several of these allegories which occur in the Ihya into his own Masnavi. Such is the famous one of the Chinese and Greek artists, which runs as follows:

"Once upon a time the Chinese having challenged the Greeks to a trial of skill in painting, the Sultan summoned them both into edifices built for the purpose directly facing each other, and commanded them to show proof of their art. The painters of the two nations immediately applied themselves with diligence to their work. The Chinese sought and obtained of the king every day a great quantity of colours, but the Greeks not the least particle. Both worked in profound silence, until the Chinese, with a clangor of cymbals and of trumpets, announced the end of their labours. Immediately the king, with his courtiers, hastened to their temple, and there stood amazed at the wonderful splendour of the Chinese painting and the exquisite beauty of the colours. But meanwhile the Greeks, who had not sought to adorn the walls with paints, but laboured rather to erase every colour, drew aside the veil which concealed their work. Then, wonderful to tell, the manifold variety of the Chinese colours was seen still more delicately and beautifully reflected from the walls of the Grecian temple, as it stood illuminated by the rays of the midday sun."

This parable, of course, illustrates the favourite Sufi tenet that the heart must he kept pure and calm as an unspotted mirror. Similarly, the epologue of the elephant in the dark (vide chap.

II.) has been borrowed by Jalaluddin Rumi from Ghazzali.

Another characteristic of Ghazzali which appeals to the, modern mind is the way in which he expounds the religious argument from probability much as Bishop Butler and Browning do (vide the end of Chapter IV. in the present book). Ghazzali might have said, with Blougram:

> *With me faith means perpetual unbelief*
> *Kept quiet like the snake 'neath Michael's foot,*
> *Who stands calm just because he feels it writhe.*

This combination of ecstatic assurance and scepticism is one of those antinomies of the human mind which annoy the rationalist and rejoice the mystic. Those in whom they coexist, like Ghazzali in the eleventh century and Cardinal Newman in the nineteenth, are a perpetual problem to understand and therefore perennially interesting:

> *He may believe, and yet, and yet,*
> *How can he?*

Another point in which Ghazzali anticipates Bishop Butler is his representation of punishment as the natural working out of consequences, and not an arbitrary infliction imposed ab extra. He tries to rationalise the lurid threatenings of the Koran.

In his own day Ghazzali was accused of having one doctrine for the multitude and one for himself and his intimate friends. Professor D. B. Macdonald, of Hartford, after going thoroughly into the matter, says, "If the charge of a secret doctrine is to be proved against Ghazzali it must be on other and better evidence than that which is now before us."

At any rate, Ghazzali has been accepted as an orthodox authority by the Muhammadans, among whom his title is *Hujjat-el-Islam* "The Proof of Islam," and it has been said, "If all the books of Islam were destroyed it would be but a slight loss if only the Ihya of Ghazzali were preserved." The great modern reformer of Islam in India, the late Sir Syud Ahmed, has had some portions of this enormous work printed separately for the purpose of familiarising the young Moslems at Aligarh with Ghazzali.

The *Ihya* was written in Arabic, and Ghazzali himself wrote an abridgment of it in Persian for popular use which he entitled *Kimiya'e Saadat* ("The Alchemy of Happiness"). This little book contains eight sections of that abridgment.

Theologians are the best judges of theologians, and in conclusion we may quote Dr. August Tholuck's opinion of Ghazzali: "This man, if ever any have deserved the name, was truly a 'divine,' and he may be justly placed on a level with Origen, so remarkable was he for learning and ingenuity, and gifted with such a rare faculty for the skilful and worthy exposition of doctrine. All that is good, noble, and sublime that his great soul had compassed he bestowed upon Muhammadanism, and he adorned the doctrines of the Koran with so much piety and learning that, in the form given them by him, they seem, in my opinion, worthy the assent of Christians. Whatsoever was most excellent in the philosophy of Aristotle or in the Sufi mysticism he discreetly adapted to the Muhammadan theology; from every school he sought the means of shedding light and honour upon religion; while his sincere piety and lofty conscientiousness imparted to all his writings a sacred majesty. He was the first of Muhammadan divines."

Angels contemplate the beauty of God, and are entirely free from animal qualities; if thou art of angelic nature, then strive towards thine origin, that thou mayest know and contemplate the Most High, and be delivered from the thraldom of lust and anger. Thou shouldest also discover why thou hast been created with these two animal instincts: whether that they should subdue and lead thee captive, or whether that thou shouldest subdue them, and, in thy upward progress, make of one thy steed and of the other thy weapon.

The first step to self-knowledge is to know that thou art composed of an outward shape, called the body, and an inward entity called the heart, or soul. By "heart" I do not mean the piece of flesh situated in the left of our bodies, but that which uses all the other faculties as its instruments and servants. In truth it does not belong to the visible world, but to the invisible, and has come into this world as a traveller visits a foreign country for the sake of merchandise, and will presently return to its native land. It is the knowledge of this entity and its attributes which is the key to the knowledge of God.

Some idea of the reality of the heart, or spirit, may be obtained by a man closing his eyes and forgetting everything around except his individuality. He will thus also obtain a glimpse of the unending nature of that individuality. Too close inquiry, however, into the essence of spirit is forbidden by the Law. In the Koran it is written: "They will question thee concerning the spirit. Say: 'The Spirit comes by the command of my Lord.'" Thus much is known of it that it is an indivisible essence belonging to the world of decrees, and that it is not from everlasting, but created. An exact philosophical knowledge of the spirit is not a necessary preliminary to walking in the path of religion, but comes rather as the result of self-discipline and perseverance in that path, as it is said in the Koran: "Those who strive in Our way, verily We will guide them to the right paths."

For the carrying on of this spiritual warfare by which the knowledge of oneself and of God is to be obtained, the body may be figured as a kingdom, the soul as its king, and the different senses and faculties as constituting an army. Reason may be called the vizier, or prime minister, passion the revenue-collector, and anger the police-officer. Under the guise of collecting revenue, passion is continually prone to plunder on its own account, while resentment is always inclined to harshness and extreme severity. Both of these, the revenue-collector and the police-officer, have to be kept in due subordination to the king, but not killed or expelled, as they have their own proper functions to fulfil. But if passion and resentment master reason, the ruin of the soul infallibly ensues. A soul which allows its lower faculties to dominate the higher is as one who should hand over an angel to the power of a dog or a Mussalman to the tyranny of an unbeliever. The cultivation of demonic, animal, or angelic qualities results in the production of corresponding characters, which in the Day of Judgment will be manifested in visible shapes, the sensual appearing as swine, the ferocious as dogs and wolves, and the pure as angels. The aim of moral discipline is to purify the heart from the rust of passion and resentment, till, like a clear mirror, it reflects the light of God.

Some one may here object, "But if man has been created with animal and demonic qualities as well as angelic, how are we to know that the latter constitute his real essence, while the former are merely accidental and transitory?" To this I answer that the essence of each creature is to be sought in that which is highest in it and peculiar to it. Thus the horse and the ass are both burden-bearing animals, but the superiority of the horse to the ass consists in its being adapted for use in battle. If it fails in this, it becomes degraded to the rank of burden-

CHAPTER II
THE KNOWLEDGE OF GOD

It is a well-known saying of the Prophet that "He who knows himself, knows God"; that is, by contemplation of his own being and attributes man arrives at some knowledge of God. But since many who contemplate themselves do not find God, it follows that there must be some special way of doing so. As a matter of fact, there are two methods of arriving at this knowledge, but one is so abstruse that it is not adapted to ordinary intelligences, and therefore is better left unexplained. The other method is as follows: When a man considers himself he knows that there was a time when he was non-existent, as it is written in the Koran: "Does it not occur to man that there was a time when he was nothing?" Further, he knows that he was made out of a drop of water in which there was neither intellect, nor hearing, sight, head, hands, feet, etc. From this it is obvious that, whatever degree of perfection he may have arrived at, he did not make himself, nor can he now make a single hair.

How much more helpless, then, was his condition when he was a mere drop of water! Thus, as we have seen in the first chapter, he finds in his own being reflected in miniature, so to speak, the power, wisdom and love of the Creator. If all the sages of the world were assembled, and their lives prolonged for an indefinite time, they could not effect any improvement in the construction of a single part of the body.

For instance, in the adaptation of the front and side-teeth to the mastication of food, and in the construction of the tongue, salivating glands, and the throat for its deglutition, we find a contrivance which cannot be improved upon. Similarly, whoever considers his hand, with its five fingers of unequal lengths, four of them with three joints and the thumb with only two, and the way in which it can be used for grasping, or for carrying, or for smiting, will frankly acknowledge that no amount of human wisdom could better it by altering the number and arrangement of the fingers, or in any other way.

When a man further considers how his various wants of food, lodging, etc., are amply supplied from the storehouse of creation, he becomes aware that God's mercy is as great as His power and wisdom, as He has Himself said, "My mercy is greater than My wrath," and according to the Prophet's saying, "God is more tender to His servants than a mother to her suckling-child." Thus from his own creation man comes to know God's existence, from the wonders of his bodily frame God's power and wisdom, and from the ample provision made for his various needs God's love. In this way the knowledge of oneself becomes a key to the knowledge of God.

Not only are man's attributes a reflection of God's attributes, but the mode of existence of man's soul affords some insight into God's mode of existence. That is to say, both God and the soul are invisible, indivisible, unconfined by space and time, and outside the categories of quantity and quality; nor can the ideas of shape, colour, or size attach to them. People find it hard to form a conception of such realities as are devoid of quality and quantity, etc., but a similar difficulty attaches to the conception of our everyday feelings, such as anger, pain, pleasure, or love. They are thought-concepts, and cannot be cognised by the senses; whereas quality, quantity, etc., are sense-concepts. Just as the ear cannot take cognisance of colour, nor the eye of sound, so, in conceiving of the ultimate realities, God and the soul, we find ourselves in a region in which sense-concepts can bear no part. So much, however, we can see, that, as God is Ruler of the universe, and, being Himself beyond space and time, quantity and quality, governs things that are so conditioned, so the soul rules the body and its members, being itself invisible, indivisible, and unlocated in any special part. For how can the indivisible be located in that which is divisible? From all this we see how true is the saying of the Prophet, "God created man in His own likeness."

And, as we arrive at some knowledge of God's essence and attributes from the contemplation of the soul's essence and attributes, so we come to understand God's method of working and government and delegation of power to angelic forces, etc., by observing how each of us governs his own little kingdom. To take a simple instance: suppose a man wishes to write the name of God. First of all the wish is conceived in his heart, it is then conveyed to the brain by the vital spirits, the form of the word "God" takes shape in the thought-chambers of the brain, thence it travels by the nerve-channels, and sets in motion the fingers, which in their turn set in motion the pen, and thus the name "God" is traced on paper exactly as it had been conceived in the writer's brain. Similarly, when God wills a thing it appears in the spiritual plane, which in the Koran is called "The Throne"[*Al Arsh*]; from the throne it passes, by a spiritual current, to a lower plane called "The Chair"[*Al Kursi*]; then the shape of it appears on the "Tablet of Destiny"[*Al Lauh Al Mahfuz*]; whence, by the mediation of the forces called "angels," it assumes actuality, and appears on the earth in the form of plants, trees, and animals, representing the will and thought of God, as the written letters represent the wish conceived in the heart and the shape present in the brain of the writer.

No one can understand a king but a king, therefore God

has made each of us a king in miniature, so to speak, over a kingdom which is an infinitely reduced copy of His own. In the, kingdom of man God's "throne" is represented by the soul, the Archangel by the heart, "the chair" by the brain, "the tablet" by the treasure-chamber of thought. The soul, itself unlocated and indivisible, governs the body as God governs the universe. In short, each of us is entrusted with a little kingdom, and charged not to be careless in the administration of it.

As regards the recognition of God's providence, there are many degrees of Knowledge. The mere physicist is like an ant who, crawling on a sheet of paper and observing black letters spreading over it, should refer the cause to the pen alone. The astronomer is like an ant of somewhat wider vision who should catch sight of the fingers moving the pen, i.e., he knows that the elements are under the power of the stars, but he does not know that the stars are under the power of the angels. Thus, owing to the different degrees of perception in people, disputes must arise in tracing effects to causes. Those whose eyes never see beyond the world of phenomena are like those who mistake servants of the lowest rank for the king. The laws of phenomena must be constant, or there could be no such thing as science; but it is a great error to mistake the slaves for the master.

As long as this difference in the perceptive faculty of observers exists, disputes must necessarily go on. It is as if some blind men, hearing that an elephant had come to their town, should go and examine it. The only knowledge of it which they can obtain comes through the sense of touch: so one handles the animal's leg, another his tusk, another his ear, and, according to their several perceptions, pronounce it to be a column, a thick pole, or a, quilt, each taking a part for the whole. So the physicist and astronomer confound the laws they perceive with the Lawgiver. A similar mistake is attributed to Abraham in the

Koran, where it is related that he turned successively to stars, moon, and sun as the objects of his worship, till grown aware of Him who made all these, he exclaimed, "I love not them that set." [1]

We have a common instance of this referring to second causes what ought to be referred to the First Cause in the case of so-called illness. For instance, if a man ceases to take any interest in worldly matters, conceives a distaste for common pleasures, and appears sunk in depression, the doctor will say, "This is a case of melancholy, and requires such and such a prescription." The physicist will say, "This is a dryness of the brain caused by hot weather and cannot be relieved till the air becomes moist." The astrologer will attribute it to some particular conjunction or opposition of planets. "Thus far their wisdom reaches," says the Koran. It does not occur to them that what has really happened is this: that the Almighty has a concern for the welfare of that man, and has therefore commanded His servants, the planets or the elements, to produce such a condition in him that he may turn away from the world to his Maker. The knowledge of this fact is a lustrous pearl from the ocean of inspirational knowledge, to which all other forms of knowledge are as islands in the sea.

The doctor, physicist, and astrologer are doubtless right each in his particular branch of knowledge, but they do not see that illness is, so to speak, a cord of love by which God draws to Himself the saints concerning whom He has said, "I was sick and ye visited Me not." Illness itself is one of those forms of experience by which man arrives at the knowledge of God, as He says by the mouth of His Prophet, "Sicknesses themselves are My servants, and are attached to My chosen."

The foregoing remarks may enable us to enter a little more fully into the meaning of those exclamations so often on the lips of the Faithful: "God is holy," "Praise be to God," "There is no God but God," "God is great." Concerning the last we may say that it does not mean that God is greater than creation, for creation is His manifestation as light manifests the sun, and it would not be correct to say that the sun is greater than its own light. It rather means that God's greatness immeasurably transcends our cognitive faculties, and that we can only form a very dim and imperfect idea of it. If a child asks us to explain to him the pleasure which exists in wielding sovereignty, we may say it is like the pleasure he feels in playing bat and ball, though in reality the two have nothing in common except that they both come under the category of pleasure. Thus, the exclamation "God is great" means that His greatness far exceeds all our powers of comprehension. Moreover, such imperfect knowledge of God as we can attain to is not a mere speculative knowledge, but must be accompanied by devotion and worship. When a man dies he has to do with God alone, and if we have to live with a person, our happiness entirely depends on the degree of affection we feel towards him. Love is the seed of happiness, and love to God is fostered and developed by worship. Such worship and constant remembrance of God implies a certain degree of austerity and curbing of bodily appetites. Not that a man is intended altogether to abolish these, for then the human race would perish. But strict limits must be set to their indulgence, and as a man is not the best judge in his own case as to what these limits should be, he had better consult some spiritual guide on the subject. Such spiritual guides are the prophets, and the laws which they have laid down under divine inspiration prescribe the limits which must be observed in these matters. He who transgresses these limits "wrongs his own soul," as it is written in the Koran.

Notwithstanding this clear pronouncement of the Koran there are those who, through their ignorance of God, do ten days!

Those who have indulged without limit in the pleasures of the world, at the time of death will be like a man who has gorged himself to repletion on delicious viands and then vomits them up. The deliciousness has gone, but the disgrace remains. The greater the abundance of the possessions which they have enjoyed in the shape of gardens, male and female slaves, gold, silver, etc., the more keenly they will feel the bitterness of parting from them. This is a bitterness which will outlast death, for the soul which has contracted covetousness as a fixed habit will necessarily in the next world suffer from the pangs of unsatisfied desire.

Another dangerous property of worldly things is that they at first appear as mere trifles, but each of these so-called "trifles" branches out into countless ramifications until they swallow up the whole of a man's time and energy. Jesus (on whom be peace!) said, "The lover of the world is like a man drinking sea-water; the more he drinks, the more thirsty he gets, till at last he perishes with thirst unquenched." The Prophet said, "You can no more mix with the world without being contaminated by it than you can go into water without getting wet."

The world is like a table spread for successive relays of guests who come and go. There are gold and silver dishes, abundance of food and perfumes. The wise guest eats as much as is sufficient for him, smells the perfumes, thanks his host, and departs. The foolish guest, on the other hand, tries to carry off some of the gold and silver dishes, only to find them wrenched out of his hands and himself thrust forth, disappointed and disgraced.

We may close these illustrations of the deceitfulness of the world with the following short parable. Suppose a ship to arrive at a certain well-wooded island. The captain of the ship tells the passengers he will stop a few hours there, and that they can go on shore for a short time, but warns them not to delay too long. Accordingly the passengers disembark and stroll in different directions. The wisest, however, return after a short time, and, finding the ship empty, choose the most comfortable places in it. A second band of the passengers spend a somewhat longer time on the island, admiring the foliage of the trees and listening to the song of the birds. Coming on board, they find the best places in the ship already occupied, and have to content themselves with the less comfortable ones. A third party wander still farther, and, finding some brilliantly coloured stones, carry them back to the ship. Their lateness in coming on board compels them to stow themselves away in the lower parts of the ship, where they find their loads of stones, which by this time have lost all their brilliancy, very much in their way. The last group go so far in their wanderings that they get quite out of reach of the captain's voice calling them to come on board, and at last he has to sail away without them. They wander about in a hopeless condition and finally either perish of hunger or fall a prey to wild beasts.

The first group represents the faithful who keep aloof from the world altogether and the last group the infidels who care only for this world and nothing for the next. The two intermediate classes are those who preserve their faith, but entangle themselves more or less with the vanities of things present.

Although we have said so much against the world, it must be remembered that there are some things in the world which are not of it, such as knowledge and good deeds. A man carries what knowledge he possesses with him into the next world, and, though his good deeds have passed, yet the effect of them remains in his character. Especially is this the case with acts of devotion, which result in the perpetual remembrance and love as to whether they had found the punishments, with which he had threatened them, real or not. When his followers asked him what was the good of questioning them, he replied, "They hear my words better than you do."

Some Sufis have had the unseen world of heaven and hell revealed to them when in a state of death-like trance. On their recovering consciousness their faces betray the nature of the revelations they have had by marks of joy or terror. But no visions are necessary to prove what will occur to every thinking man, that when death has stripped him of his senses and left him nothing but his bare personality, if while on earth he has too closely attached himself to objects perceived by the senses, such as wives, children, wealth, lands, slaves, male and female, etc., he must necessarily suffer when bereft of those objects. Whereas, on the contrary, if he has as far as possible turned his back on all earthly objects and fixed his supreme affection upon God, he will welcome death as a means of escape from worldly entanglements, and of union with Him whom he loves. In his case the Prophet's sayings will be verified:

"Death is a bridge which unites friend to friend,"
and

"The world is a paradise for infidels, but a prison for the faithful."

On the other hand, the pains which souls suffer after death all have their source in excessive love of the world. The Prophet said that. every unbeliever, after death, will be tormented by ninety-nine snakes, each having nine heads. Some simple-minded people have examined the unbelievers' graves and wondered at failing to see these snakes. They do not understand that these snakes have their abode within the unbeliever's spirit, and that they existed in him even before he died, for they were the form which he mistook for that of his bride the corpse of an old woman beginning to decay. On emerging from the mortuary with his garments all soiled, what is his shame to see his father, the king, approaching with a retinue of soldiers! Such is a feeble picture of the shame those will feel in the next world who in this have greedily abandoned themselves to what they thought were delights.

The third spiritual hell is that of disappointment and failure to reach the real objects of existence. Man was intended to mirror forth the light of the knowledge of God, but if he arrives in the next world with his soul thickly coated with the rust of sensual indulgence he will entirely fail of the object for which he was made. His disappointment may be figured in the following way: Suppose a man is passing with some companions through a dark wood. Here and there, glimmering on the ground, lie variously coloured stones. His companions collect and carry these and advise him to do the same. "For," say they "we have heard that these stones will fetch a high price in the place whither we are going." He, on the other hand, laughs at them and calls them fools for loading themselves in the vain hope of gain, while he walks free and unencumbered. Presently they emerge into the full daylight and find that these coloured stones are rubies, emeralds, and other jewels of priceless value. The man's disappointment and chagrin at not having gathered some when so easily within his reach may be more easily imagined than described. Such will be the remorse of those hereafter, who, while passing through this world, have been at no pains to acquire the jewels of virtue and the treasures of religion.

This journey of man through the world may be divided into four stages - the sensuous, the experimental, the instinctive, the rational. In the first he is like a moth which, though it has sight, has no memory, and will singe itself again and again at the same candle. In the second stage he is like a dog which, having once been beaten, will run away at the sight of a stick. In the third he is like a horse or a sheep, both of which instinctively fly at the sight of a lion or a wolf, their natural enemies, while they will not fly from a camel or a buffalo, though these last are much greater in size. In the fourth stage man altogether transcends the limits of the animals and becomes capable, to some extent, of foreseeing and providing for the future. His movements at first may be compared to ordinary walking on land, then to traversing the sea in a ship, then, on the fourth plane, where he is conversant with realities, to walking on the sea, while beyond this plane there is a fifth, known to the prophets and saints, whose progress may be compared to flying through the air.

Thus man is capable of existing on several different planes, from the animal to the angelic, and precisely in this lies his danger, i.e., of falling to the very lowest. In the Koran it is written, "We proposed the burden (i.e., responsibility or free-will) to the heavens and the earth and the mountains, and they refused to undertake it. But man took it upon himself: Verily he is ignorant." Neither animals nor, angels can change their appointed rank and place. But man may sink to the animal or soar to the angel, and this is the meaning of his undertaking that "burden" of which the Koran speaks. The majority of men choose to remain in the two lower stages mentioned above, and the stationary are always hostile to the travellers or pilgrims, whom they far outnumber.

Many of the former class, having no fixed convictions about the future world, when mastered by their sensual appetites, deny it altogether. They say that hell is merely an invention of theologians to frighten people. and they regard theologians themselves with thinly veiled contempt. To argue with fools of this kind is of very little use. This much, however, may be said to such a man, with the possible result of making him pause and reflect: "Do you really think that the hundred and twenty-four thousand [1] prophets and saints who believed in the future life were all wrong, and you are right in denying it?" If he replies, "Yes! I am as sure as I am that two are more than one, that there is no soul and no future life of joy and penalty," then the case of such a man is hopeless; all one can do is to leave him alone, remembering the words of the Koran, "Though thou call them to instruction, they will not be instructed."

But, should he say that a future life is possible but that the doctrine is so involved in doubt and mystery that it is impossible to decide whether it be true or not, then one may say to him: "Then you had better give it the benefit of the doubt! Suppose you are about to eat food and some one tells you a serpent has spat venom on it, you would probably refrain and rather endure the pangs of hunger than eat it, though your informant may be in jest or lying. Or suppose you are ill and a charm-writer says, 'Give me a, rupee and I will write a charm which you can tie round your neck and which will cure you,' you would probably give the rupee on the chance of deriving benefit from the charm. Or if an astrologer say, 'When the moon has entered a certain constellation, drink such and such a medicine, and you will recover,' though you may have very little faith in astrology, you very likely would try the experiment on the chance that he might be right. And do you not think that, reliance is as well placed on the words of all the prophets, saints, and holy men, convinced as they were of a future life, as on the promise of a charm-writer or an astrologer? People take perilous voyages in ships for the sake of merely probable profit, and will you not suffer a little pain of abstinence now for the sake of eternal joy hereafter?"

The Lord Ali once, in arguing with an unbeliever, said, "If you are right, then neither of us will be any the worse in the future; but if we are right, then we shall escape, and you will suffer." This he said not because he himself was in any doubt, but merely to make an impression on the unbeliever. From all that we have said it follows that man's chief business in this world is to prepare for the next. Even if he is doubtful about a future existence, reason suggests that he should act as if there were one, considering the tremendous issues at stake. Peace be on those who follow the instruction!

CHAPTER V

CONCERNING MUSIC AND DANCING
AS AIDS TO THE RELIGIOUS LIFE

The heart of man has been so constituted by the Almighty that, like a flint, it contains a hidden fire which is evoked by music and harmony, and renders man beside himself with ecstasy. These harmonies are echoes of that higher world of beauty which we call the world of spirits; they remind man of his relationship to that world, and produce in him an emotion so deep and strange that he himself is powerless to explain it. The effect of music and dancing is deeper in proportion as the natures on which they act are simple and prone to emotion; they fan into a flame whatever love is already dormant in the heart, whether it be earthly and sensual, or divine and spiritual.

Accordingly there has been much dispute among theologians as to the lawfulness of music and dancing regarded as religious exercises. One sect, the Zahirites,[1] holding that God is altogether incommensurable with man, deny the possibility of man's really feeling love to God, and say that he can only love those of his own species. If he does feel what he thinks is love to his Creator they say it is a mere projection, or shadow cast by his own fantasy, or a reflection of love to the creature; music and dancing, according to them, have only to do with creature love, and are therefore unlawful as religious exercises. If we ask them what is the meaning of that "love to God" which is enjoined by the religious law, they reply that it means obedience and worship. This is an error which we hope to confute in a later chapter dealing with the love of God. At present we content ourselves with saying that music and dancing do not put into the heart what is not there already, but only fan into a flame dormant emotions.

Therefore if a man has in his heart that love to God which the Law enjoins, it is perfectly lawful, nay, laudable in him to take part in exercises which promote it. On the other hand, if his heart is full of sensual desires, music and dancing will only increase them, and are therefore unlawful for him. While, if he listens to them merely as a matter of amusement, they are neither lawful nor unlawful, but indifferent. For the mere fact that they are pleasant does not make them unlawful, any more than the pleasure of listening to the singing of birds or looking at green grass and running water is unlawful. The innocent character of music and dancing, regarded merely as a pastime, is also corroborated by an authentic tradition which we have from the Lady Ayesha,[2] who narrates: "One festival-day some negroes, were performing in a mosque. The Prophet said to me, 'Do you wish to see them?' I replied, 'Yes.' Accordingly he lifted me up with his own blessed hand, and I looked on so long that he said more than once, 'Haven't you had enough'?" Another tradition from the Lady Ayesha is as follows: "One festival-day, two girls came to my house and began to play and sing. The Prophet came in and lay down on the couch, turning his face away. Presently Abu Bakr[3] entered, and, seeing the girls playing, exclaimed, 'What! the pipe of Satan in the Prophet's house!' Whereupon the Prophet turned and said, 'Let them alone, Abu Bakr, for this is a festival-day.'"

Passing over the cases where music and dancing rouse into a flame evil desires already dormant in the heart, we come to those cases where they are quite lawful. Such are those of the pilgrims who celebrate the glories of the House of God at Mecca in song, and thus incite others to go on pilgrimage, and of minstrels whose music and songs stir up martial ardour in the breasts of their auditors and incite them to fight against the infidels. Similarly, mournful music which, excites sorrow for sin and failure in the religious life is lawful; of this nature was the music of David. But dirges which increase sorrow for the dead are not lawful, for it is written in the Koran, "Despair not over what you have lost." On the other hand, joyful music at weddings and feasts and on such occasions as a circumcision or the return from a journey is lawful.

We come now to the purely religious use of music and dancing: such is that of the Sufis, who by this means stir up in themselves greater love towards God, and, by means of music, often obtain spiritual visions and ecstasies, their heart becoming in this condition as clean as silver in the flame of a furnace, and attaining a degree of purity which could never be attained by any amount of mere outward austerities. The Sufi then becomes so keenly aware of his relationship to the spiritual world that he loses all consciousness of this world, and often falls down senseless.

It is not, however, lawful for the aspirant to Sufism to take part in this mystical dancing without the permission of his "Pir," or spiritual director. It is related of the Sheikh Abu'l Qasim Girgani that, when one of his disciples requested leave to take part in such a dance, he said, "Keep a strict fast for three days; then let them cook for you tempting dishes; if, then, you still prefer the 'dance,' you may take part in it." The disciple, however, whose heart is not thoroughly purged from earthly desires, though he may have obtained some glimpse of the mystics' path, should be forbidden by his director to take part in such dances, as they will do him more harm than good.

Those who deny the reality of the ecstasies and other spiritual experiences of the Sufis merely betray their own narrow-mindedness and shallow insight. Some allowance, however, must be made for them, for it is as difficult to believe in the reality of states of which one has no personal experience as it is for a blind man to understand the pleasure of looking at green, grass and running water, or for a child to comprehend the pleasure of exercising sovereignty. A wise man, though he himself may have no experience of those states, will not therefore deny their reality, for what folly can be greater than his who denies the reality of a thing merely because he himself has not experienced it! Of such people it is written in the Koran, "Those who have not the guidance will say, 'This is a manifest imposture.'"

As regards the erotic poetry which is recited in Sufi gatherings, and to which people sometimes make objection, we must remember that, when in such poetry mention is made of separation from or union with the beloved, the Sufi, who is an adept in the love of God, applies such expressions to separation from or union with Him. Similarly, "dark locks" are taken to, signify the darkness of unbelief; "the brightness of the face," the light of faith, and drunkenness the Sufi's ecstasy. Take, for instance, the verse:

Thou may'st measure out thousands of measures of wine,
But, till thou drink it, no joy is thine.

By this the writer means that the true delights, of religion cannot be reached by way of formal instruction, but by felt attraction and desire. A man may converse much and write volumes concerning love, faith, piety, and so forth, and blacken paper to any extent, but till he himself possesses these attributes all this will do him no good. Thus, those who find fault with the Sufis for being powerfully affected, even to ecstasy, by these and similar verses, are merely shallow and uncharitable. Even camels are sometimes so powerfully affected by the Arab-songs of their drivers that they will run rapidly, bearing heavy burdens, till they fall down in a state of exhaustion.

The Sufi hearer, however, is in danger of blasphemy if he applies some of the verses which he hears to God. For instance, if he hears such a verse as "Thou art changed from thy former inclination," he must not apply it to God, who cannot change, but to himself and his own variations of mood. God is like the sun, which is always shining, but sometimes for us His light is eclipsed by some object which intervenes between us and Him.

Regarding some adepts it is related that they attain to such a degree of ecstasy that they lose themselves in God. Such was the case with Sheikh Abu'l Hassan Nuri, who, on hearing a certain verse, fell into an ecstatic condition, and, coming into a field full of stalks of newly cut sugar-canes, ran about till his feet were wounded and bleeding, and, not long afterwards, expired. In such cases some have supposed that there occurs an actual descent of Deity into humanity, but this would be as great a mistake as that of one who, having for the first time seen his reflection in a mirror, should suppose that, somehow or other, he had become incorporated with the mirror, or that the red-and-white hues which the mirror reflects were qualities inherent in it.

The states of ecstasy into which the Sufis fall vary according to the emotions which predominate in them - love, fear, desire, repentance, etc. These states, as we have mentioned above, are often the result not only of hearing verses of the Koran, but erotic poetry. Some have objected to the reciting of poetry, as well as of the Koran, on these occasions; but it should be remembered that all the verses of the Koran are not adapted to stir the emotions - such, for instance, as that which commands that a man should leave his mother the sixth part of his property and his sister the half, or that which orders that a widow must wait four months after the death of her husband before becoming espoused to another man. The natures which can be thrown in to religious ecstasy by the recital of such verses are peculiarly sensitive and very rare.

Another reason for the use of poetry as well as of the Koran on these occasions is that people are so familiar with the Koran, many even knowing it by heart, that the effect of it has been dulled by constant repetition. One cannot be always quoting new verses of the Koran as one can of poetry. Once, when some wild Arabs were hearing the Koran for the first time and were strongly moved by it, Abu-Bakr said to them, "We were once like you, but our hearts have grown hard," meaning that the Koran loses some of its effect on those familiar with it. For the same reason the Caliph Omar used to command the pilgrims to Mecca to leave it quickly, "For," he said, "I fear if you grow too familiar with the Holy City the awe of it will depart from your hearts."

There is, moreover, something pertaining to the light and frivolous, at least in the eyes of the common people, in the use of singing and musical instruments, such as the pipe and drum, and it is not befitting that the majesty of the Koran should be, even temporarily, associated with these things. It is related of the Prophet that once, when he entered the house of Rabia, the daughter of Mauz, some singing-girls who, were there began extemporising in his honour. He abruptly bade them cease, as the praise of the Prophet was too sacred a theme to be treated in that way. There is also some danger, if verses of the Koran are exclusively used, that, the hearers should attach to them some private interpretation of their own, and this is unlawful. On the other hand, no harm attaches to interpreting lines of poetry in various ways, as it is not necessary to apply to a poem the same meaning which the author had.

Other features of these mystic dances are the bodily contortions and tearing of clothes with which they are sometimes accompanied. If these are the result of genuine ecstatic conditions there is nothing to be said against them, but if they are self-conscious and deliberate on the part of those who wish to appear "adepts," then they are merely acts of hypocrisy. In any case the more perfect adept is he who controls himself till he is absolutely obliged to give vent to his feelings. It is related of a certain youth who was a disciple of the Sheikh Junaid that, on hearing singing commence in an assembly of the Sufis, he could not restrain himself, but began to shriek in ecstasy. Junaid said to him, "If you do that again, don't remain in my company." After this the youth used to restrain himself on such occasions, but at last one, day his emotions were so powerfully stirred that, after long and forcible repression of them, he uttered a shriek and died.

To conclude: in holding these assemblies, regard must be had to time and place, and that no spectators come from unworthy motives. Those who participate in them should sit in silence, not looking at one another, but keeping their heads bent, as at prayer, and concentrating their minds on God. Each should watch for whatever may be revealed to his own heart, and not make any movements from mere self-conscious impulse. But if any one of them stands up in a state of genuine ecstasy all the rest should stand up with him, and if any one's turban fall off the others should also lay their turbans down.

Although these matters are comparative novelties in Islam and have not been received from the first followers of the Prophet, we must remember that all novelties are not forbidden, but only those which directly contravene the Law. For instance, the "Tarawih," or night-prayer, was first instituted by the Caliph Omar. The Prophet said, "Live with each man according to his habits and disposition," therefore it is right to fall in with usages that please people, when non-conformity would vex them. It is true that the Companions were not in the habit of rising on the entrance of the Prophet, as they disliked this practice; but where it has become established, and abstaining from it would cause annoyance, it is better to conform to it. The Arabs have their own customs, and the Persians have theirs, and God knoweth which is best.

CHAPTER VI

CONCERNING SELF-EXAMINATION AND THE
RECOLLECTION OF GOD

Know, O brother, that in the Koran God hath said, "We will set up a just balance on the day of resurrection, and no soul shall be wronged in anything." Whosoever has wrought a grain of good or ill shall then behold it. In the Koran it is also written, "Let every soul see what it sends on before it for the day of account." It was a saying of the Caliph Omar's, "Call yourselves to account before ye be called to account"; and God says, "O ye believers, be patient and strive against your natural desires, and maintain the strife manfully." The saints have always understood that they have come into this world to carry on a spiritual traffic, the resulting gain or loss of which is heaven or hell. They have, therefore, always kept a jealous eye upon the flesh, which, like a treacherous partner in business, may cause them great loss. He, therefore, is a wise man who, after his morning prayer, spends a whole hour in making a spiritual reckoning, and says to his soul, "O my soul, thou hast only one life; no single moment that has passed can be recovered, for in the counsel of God the number of breaths allotted thee is fixed, and cannot be increased. When life is over no further spiritual traffic is possible for thee; therefore what thou dost, do now; treat this day as if thy life had been already spent, and this were an extra day granted thee by the special favour of the Almighty, What can be greater folly than to lose it?"

At the resurrection a man will find all the hours of his life arranged like a long series of treasure-chests. The door of one will be opened, and it will be seen to be full of light: it represents an hour which he spent in doing good. His heart will be filled which such joy that even a fraction of it would make the inhabitants of hell forget the fire. The door of a second will be opened; it is pitch-dark within, and from it issues such an evil odour as will cause every one to hold his nose: it represents an hour which he spent in ill-doing, and he will suffer such terror that a fraction of it would embitter Paradise for the blessed. The door of a third treasure-chest will be opened; it will be seen to, be empty and neither light nor dark within: this represents the hour in which he did neither good nor evil. Then he will feel remorse and confusion like that of a man who has been the possessor of a great treasure and wasted it or let it slip from his grasp. Thus the whole, series of the hours of his life will be displayed, one by one, to his gaze. Therefore a man should, say to his soul every morning, "God has given thee twenty-four treasures; take heed lest thou lose any one of them., for thou wilt not be able to endure the regret that will follow such loss."

The saints have said, "Even suppose God should forgive thee, after a wasted life, thou wilt not attain to the ranks of the righteous and must deplore thy loss; therefore keep a strict watch over thy tongue, thine eye, and each of thy seven members, for each of these is, as it, were, a possible gate to hell. Say to thy flesh, 'If thou art rebellious, verily I will punish thee'; for, though the flesh is headstrong, it is capable of receiving instruction, and can be tamed by austerity." Such, then, is the aim of self-examination, and the Prophet had said, "Happy is he who does now that which will benefit him after death."

We come now to the recollection of God. This consists in a man's remembering that God observes all his acts and thoughts. People only see the outward, while God sees both the outer and the inner man. He who really believes this will have both his outer and inner being well disciplined. If he disbelieve it, he is an infidel, and if, while believing it, he acts contrary to that belief, be is guilty of the grossest. presumption. One day a negro came to the Prophet and said, "O Prophet of God! I have committed much sin. Will my repentance be accepted, or not?" The Prophet said "Yes." Then the negro said, "O Prophet of God, all the time I was committing sin, did God really behold it?" "Yes," was the answer. The negro uttered a cry and fell lifeless. Till a man is thoroughly convinced of the fact that be is always under God's observation it is impossible for him to act rightly.

A certain sheikh once had a disciple whom he favoured above his other disciples, thus exciting their envy. One day the sheikh gave each of them a fowl and told each to go and kill it in a place where no one could see him. Accordingly each killed his fowl in some retired spot and brought it back, with the exception of the sheikh's favourite disciple, who brought his back alive, saying, "I have found no such place, for God sees everywhere." The sheikh said to the others, "You see now this youth's real rank; he has attained to the constant remembrance of God."

When Zuleikha tempted Joseph she cast a cloth over the face of the idol she used to worship. Joseph said to her, "O Zuleikha, thou art ashamed before a block of stone, and should I not be ashamed before Him who created the seven heavens and the earth?" A man once came to the saint Junaid and said, "I cannot keep my eyes from casting lascivious looks. How shall I do so?" "By remembering," Junaid answered, "that God sees you much more clearly than you see any one else." In the traditions it is written that God has said, "Paradise is for those who intend to commit some sin and then remember that My eye is upon them and forbear." Abdullah Ibn Dinar relates, "Once I was walking with the Caliph Omar near Mecca when we met a shepherd's slave-boy driving his flock. Omar said to him, "Sell me a sheep." The boy answered, "They are not mine, but my master's." Then, to try him, Omar said, "Well, you can tell him that a wolf carried one off, and he will know nothing about it." "No, he won't," said the boy, "but God will." Omar then wept, and, sending for the boy's master, purchased him and set him free, exclaiming, "For this saying thou art free in this world and shalt be free in the next."

There are two degrees of this recollection of God. The first degree is that of those saints whose thoughts are altogether absorbed in the contemplation of the majesty of God, and have no room in their hearts for anything else at all. This is the lower degree of recollection, for when a man's heart is fixed, and his limbs are so controlled by his heart that they abstain from even lawful actions, he has no need of any device or safeguard against sins. It was to this kind of recollection that the Prophet referred when he said, "He who rises in the morning with only God in his mind, God shall look after him, both in this world and the next."

Some of these recollectors of God are so absorbed in the thought of Him that, if people speak to them they do not hear, or walk in front of them they do not see, but stumble as if they collided with a wall. A certain saint relates as follows: "One day I passed by a place where archers were having a shooting-match. Some way off a man was sitting alone. I approached him and attempted to engage him in talk, but he replied, "The remembrance of God is better than talk." I said, "Are you not lonely?" "No," he answered, "God and two angels are with me." Pointing to the archers, I asked, Which of these has carried off the prize?" "That one," was his reply, "to whom God has

and discrimination are closely connected, and he in whom reason does not rule passion will not be keen to discriminate.

Besides such cautious discrimination, before acting a man should call himself strictly to account for his past actions. Every evening he should examine his heart as to what he has done to see whether he has gained or lost in his spiritual capital. This is the more necessary as the heart is like a treacherous business partner, always ready to cajole and deceive; sometimes it presents its own selfishness under the guise of obedience to God, so that a man supposes he has gained, whereas he has really lost.

A certain saint named Amiya, sixty years of age, counted up the days of his life. He found they amounted to twenty-one thousand six hundred days. He said to himself, "Alas! if I have committed one sin every day, how can I escape from the load of twenty-one thousand six hundred sins?" He uttered a cry and fell to the ground; when they came to raise him they found him dead. But most people are heedless, and never think of calling themselves to account. If for every sin a man committed he placed a stone in an empty house, he would soon find that house full of stones; if his recording angels[3] demanded wages of him for writing down his sins, all his money would soon be gone. People count on their rosaries[4] with self-satisfaction the numbers of times they have recited the name of God, but they keep no rosary for reckoning the numberless idle words they speak. Therefore the Caliph Omar said, "Weigh well your words and deeds before they be weighed at the Judgment." He himself before retiring for the night, used to strike his feet with a scourge and exclaim, "What hast thou done to-day?" Abu Talha was once praying in a palm-grove, when the sight of a beautiful bird which flew out of it caused him to make a mistake in counting the number of prostrations he had made. To punish himself for his inattention, he gave the palm-grove away. Such saints knew that their sensual nature was prone to go astray, therefore they kept a strict watch over it, and punished it for each transgression.

If a man finds himself sluggish and averse from austerity and self-discipline he should consort with one who is a proficient in such practices so as to catch the contagion of his enthusiasm. One saint used to say, "When I grow lukewarm in self-discipline, I look at Muhammad Ibn Wasi, and the sight of him rekindles my fervour for at least a week." If one cannot find such a pattern of austerity close at hand, then it is a good thing to study the lives of the saints; he should also exhort his soul somewhat in the following way: "O my soul! thou thinkest thyself intelligent and art angry at being called a fool, and yet what else art thou, after all? Thou preparest clothing to shield thee from the cold of winter, yet makest no preparation for the after-life. Thy state is like that of a man who in mid-winter should say, 'I will wear no warm clothing, but trust to God's mercy to shield me from the cold. He forgets that God, at the same time that He created cold, showed man the way to make clothing to protect himself from it, and provided the material for that clothing. Remember this also, O soul, that thy punishment hereafter will not be because God is angry with thy disobedience;. and say not, 'How can my sin hurt God?' It is thy lusts themselves which will have kindled the flames of a hell within thee; just as, from eating unwholesome food, disease is caused in a man's body, and not because his doctor is vexed with him for disobeying his orders.

"Shame upon thee, O soul, for thy overweening love of the world! If thou dost not believe in heaven or hell, at any rate thou believes in death, which will snatch from thee all worldly delights and cause thee to feel the pangs of separation from them, which will be intenser just in proportion as thou hast attached thyself to them. Why art thou mad after the world? If the whole of it, from East to West, were thine and worshipped thee, yet it would all, in a brief space, turn to dust along with thyself, and oblivion would blot out thy name, as those of ancient kings before thee. But now, seeing thou hast only a very small fragment of the world, and that a defiled one, wilt thou be so mad as to barter eternal joy for it, a precious jewel for a broken cup of earthenware, and make thyself the laughingstock of all around thee?"

CHAPTER VII

MARRIAGE AS A HELP OR HINDRANCE
TO THE RELIGIOUS LIFE

Marriage plays such a large part in human affairs that it must necessarily be taken into account in treating of the religious lifer and be regarded in both its aspects of advantage and disadvantage.

Seeing that God, as the Koran says, "only created men and genii for the purpose of worshipping," the first and obvious advantage of marriage is that the worshippers of God may increase in number. Theologians have therefore laid it down as a maxim that it is better to be engaged in matrimonial duties than in supererogatory devotions.

Another advantage of marriage is that, as the Prophet said, the prayers of children profit their parents when the latter are dead, and children who die before their parents intercede for them on the Day of Judgment. "When a child," said the Prophet, "is told to enter heaven, it weeps and says, 'I will not enter in without my father and mother.'" Again, one day the Prophet seized hold of a man's sleeves and drew him violently towards himself, saying, "Even thus shall children draw their parents into heaven." He added, "Children crowd together at the gate of heaven and cry out for their fathers and mothers, till those of the latter who are outside are told to enter in and join their children."

It is related of a certain celibate saint that he once dreamt

be brought forward and stationed near the Balance.[1] He will then be asked, "'By what means did you support your family?' He will not be able to give a satisfactory answer, and all his good works will be cancelled, and proclamation will be made concerning him, 'This is the man whose family have devoured all his good deeds!'"

Another drawback to marriage is this, that to treat one's family kindly and patiently and to bring their affairs to a satisfactory issue can only be done by those who have a good disposition. There is great danger lest a man should treat his family harshly, or neglect them, and so bring sin upon himself. The Prophet said: "He who deserts his wife and children is like a runaway slave; till he returns to them none of his fasts or prayers will be accepted by God." In brief, man has a lower nature, and, till he can control his own lower nature, he had better not assume the responsibility of controlling another's. Some one asked the saint Bishr Hafi why he did not marry. "I am afraid," he replied, "of that verse in the Koran, "The rights of women over men are precisely the same as the rights of men over women.'"

A third disadvantage of marriage is that the cares of a family often prevent a man from concentrating his thoughts on God and on a future life, and may, unless he is careful, lead to his destruction, for God has said, "Let not your wives and children turn you away from remembering God." He who thinks he can concentrate himself better on his religious duties by not marrying had better remain single, and he who fears falling into sin if he does not marry, had better do so.

We now come to the qualities which should be sought in a wife. The most important of all is chastity. If a wife is unchaste, and her husband keeps silent, he gets a bad name and is hindered in his religious life; if he speaks, his life becomes embittered;

and if he divorces her, he may feel the pang of separation. A wife who is beautiful but of evil character is a great calamity; such a one had better be divorced.

The Prophet said, "He who seeks a wife for the sake of her beauty or wealth will lose both."

The second desirable quality in a wife is a good disposition. An ill-tempered or ungrateful or loquacious or imperious wife makes existence unbearable, and is a great hindrance to leading a devout life.

The third quality to be sought is beauty, as this calls forth love and affection. Therefore one should see a woman before marrying her. The Prophet said, "The women of such a tribe have all a defect in their eyes; he who wishes, to marry one should see her first." The wise have said that he who marries a wife without seeing her is sure to repent it afterwards. It is true that one should not marry solely for the sake of beauty, but this does not mean that beauty should be reckoned of no account at all.

The fourth desirable point is that the sum paid by the husband as the wife's marriage-portion should be moderate. The Prophet said, "She is the best kind of wife whose marriage-portion is small, and whose beauty is great."

He himself settled the marriage-portion of some women at ten dirhems,[2] and his own daughters' marriage-portions were not more than four hundred dirhems.

Fifthly, she should not be barren. "A piece of old matting lying in the corner of the house is better than a barren wife." [3]

Other qualities in a desirable wife are these: she should be of a good stock, not married previously, and not too nearly related to her husband.

Regarding the Observances of Marriage

Marriage is a religious institution, and should be treated in a religious way, otherwise the mating of men and women is no better than the mating of animals. The Law enjoins that there should be a feast on the occasion of every marriage. When Abdurrahman Ibn Auf married, the Prophet said to him, "Make a marriage-feast, even if you have only a goat to make it with." When the Prophet himself celebrated his marriage with Safia he made a marriage-feast of dates and barley. It is also right that. marriage should be accompanied with the beating of drums and of music, for man is the crown of creation.

Secondly, a man should remain on good terms with his wife. This does not mean that he should never cause her pain, but that he should bear any annoyance she causes him, whether by her unreasonableness or ingratitude, patiently. Woman is created weak, and requiring concealment; she should therefore be borne with patiently, and kept secluded. The Prophet said, "He who bears the ill-humour of his wife patiently will earn as much merit as Job did by the patient endurance of his trials." On his, death-bed also he was heard to say, "Continue in prayer and treat your wives well, for they are your prisoners." He himself used to bear patiently the tempers of his wives. One day Omar's wife was angry and scolded him. He said to her, "Thou evil-tongued one, dost thou answer me back?" She replied, "Yes! the Lord of the prophets is better than thou, and his wives, answer him back." He replied, "Alas for Hafsa [Omar's daughter and Muhammad's wife] if she does not humble herself"; and when he met her he said, "Take care not to answer the Prophet back." The Prophet also said, "The best of you is he who is best to his own family, as I am the best to mine."

Thirdly, a man should condescend to his wife's recreations

hell or hope of heaven? If I had created neither, should I not then have deserved to be worshipped?"

The fourth cause of this love is the affinity between man and God, which is referred to in the saying of the Prophet, "Verily God created man in His own likeness." Furthermore, God has said, "My servant seeks proximity to Me, that I may make him My friend, and when I have made him My friend I become his ear, his eye, his tongue." Again, God said to Moses, "I was sick, and thou didst not visit Me?" Moses replied, "O God! Thou art Lord of heaven and earth: how couldest Thou be sick?" God said, "A certain servant of Mine was sick; hadst thou visited him, thou wouldst have visited Me."

This is a somewhat dangerous topic to dwell upon, as it is beyond the understanding of common people, and even intelligent men have stumbled in treating of it, and come to believe in incarnation and union with God. Still, the affinity which does exist between man and God disposes of the objection of those theologians mentioned above, who maintain that man cannot love a Being who is not of his own species. However great the distance between them, man can love God because of the affinity indicated in the saying, "God created man in His own likeness."

The Vision of God

All Moslems profess to believe that the Vision of God is the summit of human felicity, because it is so stated in the Law; but with many this is a mere lip-profession which arouses no emotion in their hearts. This is quite, natural, for how can a man long for a thing of which he has no knowledge? We will endeavour to show briefly why the Vision of God is the greatest happiness to which a man can attain.

In the first place, every one of man's faculties has its appropriate function which it delights to fulfil. This holds good of them all, from the lowest bodily appetite to the highest form of intellectual apprehension. But even a comparatively low form of mental exertion affords greater pleasure than the satisfaction of bodily appetites. Thus, if a man happens to be absorbed in a game of chess, he will not come to his meal, though repeatedly summoned. And the higher the subject-matter of our knowledge, the greater is our delight in it; for instance, we would take more pleasure in knowing the secrets of a king than the secrets of a vizier. Seeing, then, that God is the highest possible object of knowledge, the knowledge of Him must afford more delight than any other. He who knows God, even in this world, dwells, as it were, in a paradise, "the breadth of which is as the breadth of the heavens and the earth,"[3] a paradise the fruits of which no envy can prevent him plucking, and the extent of which is not narrowed by the multitude of those who occupy it.

But the delight of knowledge still falls short of the delight of vision, just as our pleasure in thinking of those we love is much less than the pleasure afforded by the actual sight of them. Our imprisonment in bodies of clay and water, and entanglement in the things of sense constitute a veil which hides the Vision of God from us, although it does not prevent our attaining to some knowledge of Him. For this reason God said to Moses on Mount Sinai, "Thou shalt not see Me."[4]

The truth of the matter is this, that, just as the seed of man becomes a man, and a buried datestone becomes a palm-tree, so the knowledge of God acquired on earth will in the next world change into the Vision of God, and he who has never learnt the knowledge will never have the Vision. This Vision will not be shared alike by all who know, but their discernment of it will vary exactly as their knowledge. God is one, but He will be seen in many different ways, just as one object is reflected in different ways by different mirrors, some showing it straight, and some distorted, some clearly and some dimly. A mirror may be so crooked as to make even a beautiful form appear misshapen, and a man may carry into the next world a heart so dark and distorted that the sight which will be a source of peace and joy to others will be to him a source of misery. He, in whose heart the love of God has prevailed over all else, will derive more joy from this vision than he in whose heart it has not so prevailed; just as in the case of two men with equally powerful eyesight, gazing on a beautiful face, he who already loves the possessor of that face will rejoice in beholding it more than he who does not. For perfect happiness mere knowledge is not enough, unaccompanied by love, and the love of God cannot take possession of a man's heart till it be purified from love of the world, which purification can only be effected by abstinence and austerity. While he is in this world a man's condition with regard to the Vision of God is like that of a lover who should see his Beloved's face in the twilight, while his clothes are infested with hornets and scorpions, which continually torment him. But should the sun arise and reveal his Beloved's face in all its beauty, and the noxious vermin leave off molesting him, then the lover's joy will be like that of God's servant, who, released from the twilight and the tormenting trials of this world, beholds Him without a veil. Abu Suleiman said, "He who is busy with himself now will be busy with himself then, and he who is occupied with God now will be occupied with Him then."

Yahya Ibn Muaz relates, "I watched Bayazid Bistami at prayer through one entire night. When he had finished he stood up and said, 'O Lord! some of Thy servants have asked and obtained of Thee the power to perform miracles, to walk on the sea, and to fly in the air, but this I do not ask; some have asked and obtained treasures, but these I do not ask.' Then he turned, and, seeing me, said, 'Are you there, Yahya?' I replied, 'Yes.' He asked, 'Since when? I answered, 'For a long time.' I then asked him to reveal to me some of his spiritual experiences. 'I will reveal,' he answered, 'what is lawful to tell you. The Almighty showed me His kingdom, from its loftiest to its lowest; He raised me above the throne and the seat and all the seven heavens. Then He said, "Ask of me whatsoever thing thou desirest." I answered, "Lord! I wish for nothing beside Thee." '"Verily," He said, "thou art My servant.'"

On another occasion Bayazid said, "Were God to offer thee the intimacy with Himself of Abraham, the power in prayer of Moses, the spirituality of Jesus, yet keep thy face directed to Him only, for He has treasures surpassing even these." One day a friend said to him, "For thirty years I have fasted by day and prayed by night and have found none of that spiritual joy of which thou speakest." Bayazid answered, "If you fasted and prayed for three hundred years, you would never find it." "How is that?" asked the other. "Because," said Bayazid, "your selfishness is acting as a veil between you and God." "Tell me, then, the cure." "It is a cure which you cannot carry out." However, as his friend pressed him to reveal it, Bayazid said, "Go to the nearest barber and have your beard shaved; strip yourself of your clothes, with the exception of a girdle round your loins. Take a horse's nosebag full of walnuts, hang it round your neck, go into the bazaar and cry out, 'Any boy who gives me a slap on the nape of my neck shall have a walnut.' Then, in this manner, go where the Cadi and the doctors of the law are sitting." "Bless my soul!" said his friend, "I really can't do that; do suggest some other remedy." "This is the indispensable preliminary to a cure," answered Bayazid, "but, as I told you, you are incurable."

The reason Bayazid indicated this method of cure for want of relish in devotion was that his friend was an ambitious seeker after place and honour. Ambition and pride are diseases which can only be cured in some such way. God said unto Jesus, "O Jesus! when I see in My servants' hearts pure love for Myself unmixed with any selfish desire concerning this world or the next, I act as guardian over that love." Again, when people asked Jesus "What is the highest work of all?" he answered,

Parchment Books is committed to publishing high quality Esoteric/Mystic classic texts at a reasonable price.

With the premium on space in modern dwellings, we also strive - within the limits of good book design - to make our products as slender as possible, allowing more books to be fitted into a given bookshelf area.

Parchment Books is an imprint of Aziloth Books, which has established itself as a publisher boasting a diverse list of powerful, quality titles, including novels of flair and originality, and factual publications on controversial issues that have not found a home in the rather staid and politically-correct atmosphere of many publishing houses.

Titles Include:

Secret Doctrines of the Rosicrucians	Magus Incognito
Corpus Hermeticum	GRS Mead (trans.)
The Virgin of the World	Hermes Trismegistus
Raja Yoga	Yogi Ramacharaka
Knowledge of the Higher Worlds	Steiner
The Outline of Sanity	GK Chesterton
The Most Holy Trinosophia	St Germaine
The Gospel of Thomas	Anonymous
Pistis Sophia	GRS Mead (trans.)

Obtainable at all good online and local bookstores.
View Aziloth's full list at:

www.azilothbooks.com

We are a small, approachable company and would love to hear any of your comments and suggestions on our plans, products, or indeed on absolutely anything.   Aziloth is also interested in hearing from aspiring authors whom we might publish. We look forward to meeting you.

Contact us at: info@azilothbooks.com.

CATHEDRAL CLASSICS

Parchment Book's sister imprint, Cathedral Classics, hosts an array of classic literature, from ancient tomes to twentieth-century masterpieces, all of which deserve a place in your home. A small selection is detailed below:

Mary Shelley	*Frankenstein*
H G Wells	*The Time Machine; The Invisible Man*
Niccolo Machiavelli	*The Prince*
Omar Khayyam	*The Rubaiyat of Omar Khayyam*
Joseph Conrad	*Heart of Darkness; The Secret Agent*
Jane Austen	*Persuasion; Northanger Abbey*
Oscar Wilde	*The Picture of Dorian Gray*
Voltaire	*Candide*
Bulwer Lytton	*The Coming Race*
Arthur Conan Doyle	*The Adventures of Sherlock Holmes*
John Buchan	*The Thirty-Nine Steps*
Friedrich Nietzsche	*Beyond Good and Evil*
Henry James	*Washington Square*
Stephen Crane	*The Red Badge of Courage*
Ralph Waldo Emmerson	*Self-Reliance, & Other Essays (series 1&2)*
Sun Tzu	*The Art of War*
Charles Dickens	*A Christmas Carol*
Fyodor Dostoyevsky	*The Gambler; The Double*
Virginia Wolf	*To the Lighthouse; Mrs Dalloway*
Johann W Goethe	*The Sorrows of Young Werther*
Walt Whitman	*Leaves of Grass - 1855 edition*
Confucius	*Analects*
Anonymous	*Beowulf*
Anne Bronte	*Agnes Grey*
More	*Utopia*

full list at: www.azilothbooks.com

Obtainable at all good online and local bookstores.

THE CARTON CHRONICLES

THE CURIOUS TALE OF
FLASHMAN'S TRUE FATHER

Keith Laidler

Morose, cynical and given to drink, Sydney Carton is one of Charles Dickens' most famous characters; a cold, dispassionate man, yet capable, in the final moments of A Tale of Two Cities, of sacrificing himself beneath the guillotine for Lucie, the woman he both loved and lost.

It now appears, however, that Dickens was being somewhat economical with the actualité.

Newly recovered documents, written in Carton's own hand, tell a far different tale. Sydney Carton survived his execution, only to find himself at the mercy of the monstrous Robespierre, author of the Paris Terror. His love Lucie languishes in a French prison, her husband dead, and Carton can ensure her survival only by becoming Robespierre's personal spy.

Reluctant, terrified and often drunk, Carton blunders his way through the major events of the French Revolution, grudgingly partaking in some of the blackest deeds of the Terror and, by a mixture of cowardice, bravado and luck, lending a hand in the fall of most of its leading figures. Kidnapped by the British, he finds himself a double agent, trusted by neither side. Our hero chronicles the slow decay of revolutionary ideals and, in passing, casts light on the true parentage of that sadistic villain of "Tom Brown's Schooldays", the beastly Flashman.

Praise for Keith Laidler's writing:

"Laidler's book is meticulously researched and covers a fascinating period" (The Times)

"It is a riveting story, and Laidler tells it well" (Sunday Telegraph Review)

From all good online and local bookstores.